Praise for
I Can Pray Every Day

"I can totally see little children reading this book in sacrament meetings all over the world. It captivated and excited me to teach my little ones to say the words 'I can pray every day.' Christensen and Egbert give your little ones a powerful and uplifting message on praying every day to enjoy anytime and anywhere."

—Annalisa Hall
bestselling LDS children's author

"Colorful and fun to read, *I Can Pray Every Day* shows children all the different reasons to pray to their Heavenly Father. This is a book I will read to my kids again and again."

—Heidi Poelman
author of *A Is for Abinadi* and *A Mother's Greatest Gift*

"One of the most important things someone can teach a child about is prayer. In *I Can Pray Every Day*, the simple messages about prayer, captured with fun illustrations, will not only help children learn about prayer but also help parents teach about prayer. What a great book for bedtime, family home evenings, and primary lessons. Every parent and teacher should have this wonderful book in their teaching tool box!"

—Mark Nielsen
author of *I Believe in Jesus Too*

To Jon, who told me to write this book, and
to Juliette as we teach you to pray.
—Catherine Christensen

To Catherine Christensen, Shawnda Craig,
and Emily Chambers. Thanks for putting up
with me and being just great to work with.
—Corey Egbert

Text © 2015 Catherine Christensen
Illustrations © 2015 Corey Egbert

ISBN 978-1-4621-1646-1

Published by CFI, an imprint of Cedar Fort, Inc.
2373 W. 700 S., Springville, UT 84663
Distributed by Cedar Fort, Inc., www.cedarfort.com

Library of Congress Control Number: 2015933251

Cover and interior layout design by Shawnda T. Craig
Cover design © 2015 Lyle Mortimer
Edited by Jessica B. Ellingson

Printed in China

10 9 8 7 6 5 4 3 2 1

I Can Pray Every Day

Written by Catherine Christensen

Illustrated by Corey Egbert

CFI
An Imprint of Cedar Fort, Inc.
Springville, Utah

I can pray.
I can pray every day.

I pray with all my family,
At daily prayers and FHE.

I pray at church

or at my school,

The park,

the store,

even the pool!

I've learned
to bless the
food I eat,

Like breakfast,
lunch, or
yummy treat!

Family, toys, my little kitten.

I can pray to help another—

Grandma, friends, or older brother.

glad
or
sad

I pray
when I am

And ask forgiveness if I'm bad.

or clean
the yard.

Heavenly Father
hears my prayers.
I know He listens
and He cares.

He hears no matter what I say.
He hears me ANYTIME I pray!

About the Author

Catherine loves books. She reads books, writes books, edits books, collects books, and even shelved books at the library for her first job. She also loves to travel and explore the world with her husband, Jon, and her daughter, Juliette. Catherine earned her BA from Brigham Young University. She grew up in England and now lives in Springville, Utah.

About the Illustrator

Corey Egbert has illustrated over ten books for children and numerous other publications. He has also exhibited his work in galleries and won awards for his handmade prints and digital illustrations. He lives in the beautiful Shenandoah Valley of Virginia with his wife, his son, and their orange tabby.